Jobs don't always go to the most qualified

...they go to the most prepared

**Writing Resumes to obtain the Interview
(30 samples)**

**Writing Cover Letters
(samples)**

**The Salary History
(samples)**

Filling out the Application

The Interview

**The 'Thank You' letter
(sample)**

AuthorHouse™
1663 Liberty Drive, Suite 200
Bloomington, IN 47403
www.authorhouse.com
Phone: 1-800-839-8640

First published by AuthorHouse 7/1/2009

ISBN: 978-1-4389-6059-3 (e)
ISBN: 978-1-4389-6058-6 (sc)

Printed in the United States of America
Bloomington, Indiana

This book is printed on acid-free paper.

Library of Congress Control Number: 2009903935

authorHOUSE®

Contents

Resumes are necessary documents to secure the interview

During my business career, I have read many resumes, cover letters and interviewed many prospective employees. I have provided guidance and counsel to many people in the proper and successful way to develop resumes and cover letters.

On developing the resumes, I contacted many employers (large and small) and asked them what they wanted to read in a resume. They wanted a resume: which could be read in 10-15 seconds; a chronological resume which could be scanned; no more than 2 pages on white 81/2" x 11" paper - no staples; if mailed, do not fold – send in a large envelope; no fancy type fonts or pictures; a cover letter should be sent with the resume summarizing the skills, experiences and education.

Due to the request of many unemployed people, I developed a workshop for white and blue-collar workers, which was presented throughout the state. In addition, presentations were made to management clubs, schools, and other organizations.

The application and interviews are products of the resume and cover letter. It is important that the resume and application coincide with the interview.

It is much easier to obtain that new job when you are employed.

IT WORKS

Below are letters received from workshop attendees who followed the resume and cover letter formats:

….."the three-job selection guided my job search and reduced the time of unemployment. Secondly, the training I received on resume writing was invaluable. I mailed less than ten resumes, received three first time interviews and two invitations for a second interview. Most importantly, <u>I got the job!</u>"

P. H., Indianapolis, Indiana

….."thank you for helping me create a powerful resume and cover letter that produced unspeakable results. Within days of sending my resumes, employers were calling me for interviews".

J. H., Indianapolis, Indiana

….."thank you for assisting me with my first resume after graduating from college as a teacher. Having only teaching theory with little practical knowledge, you provided the guidance in producing a resume and cover letter, which resulted in my being immediately hired. Thank you again, for your assistance".

M. G., Lancaster, Ohio

Jobs don't always go to the most qualified

...they go to the most prepared

Developing the Resume

First, you must have a signature block at the top of the page to include your name (larger than other print and in Arial bold 14 point caps). The address, phone number and email address will be in 12 point Arial. I recommend using Arial type font as it is easy to read and scanned. No abbreviations. The email address may be placed at the signature block or on the cover letter. All should be centered:

JANE or JOHN DOE
123 Main Street
AnyTown, AnyState AnyZip
000-000-0000
email@abc.com

Second, you must decide what job you want to apply for – based on your skills, experience and education. There may be more than one.

Typically, there are seven business disciplines from which to apply:

1. Administrative: President; Vice-President; Control Department (Accounting); Human Resources; Quality Control.
2. Engineering; Research and Development.
3. Manufacturing – CNC Machine Operator;

        Tool & Die Maker; Maintenance Mechanic.

4. **Production – Assembling; Purchasing; Warehousing.**
5. **Product Management; Marketing.**
6. **Sales.**
7. **Information Technology (IT); and Service – If the company services their own manufactured or OEM products.**

In small businesses, you would want to contact the president or owner. S/he typically manages all of the above functions.

Your job objective is targeted to the position to which you are applying, ie:

OBJECTIVE: To interview for the position of **Buyer**

To ensure a sharp margin, use the tab key rather than the space bar.

If you are unsure which job you would be best suited, I would suggest your going to your state employment department and speak to an employment counselor. They will test you to determine which areas of employment you are best qualified. These services are typically free.

If you are interested in starting a new career, check with the Department of Labor, Bureau of Apprenticeship and Training (BAT). This federal

government agency approves training programs throughout the country, typically with large organizations and the building trades. These programs will pay and educate you as you learn. Typically, benefits are provided. At the end of training, the apprentice becomes a journeyworker and is recognized throughout the United States.

Next, develop your chronological work skills and experiences. Companies typically want you to go back at least 10 or more years. An example would be:

Jan 97 to
Present:

ABC Company, Greensburg, Indiana
BUYER: Source, secure bids and purchase raw materials for manufacturing. Source subassemblies and coordinated with engineering and quality control to determine if materials are to specifications. Monitor stock levels at distribution centers. Maintain stock levels at production control. Submit reports.

If you have worked with a company and have held multiple positions, this shows upward mobility and is beneficial to your resume. Format your experiences as shown:

Jan 97 to
Present

ABC Company, Greensburg, Indiana
BUYER: Source, secure bids and purchase raw materials for manufacturing. Source subassemblies and coordinate with engineering and quality control to determine if materials are to specifications. Monitor stock levels at distribution centers. Maintain stock levels at production control. Submit reports.

WAREHOUSE SUPERVISOR: Received production subassemblies as documented on purchase orders and specifications. Coordinate with quality control and production control. Directed forklift operators to stage at production lines. Maintain min/max stock systems and communicate to purchasing. Operate computer. Monitor maintenance on equipment.

If a temporary agency has placed you in a temporary position, list your position as:

Jan 07 to   HIJ Company, Seymour, Indiana.
Present   **WAREHOUSE WORKER (Temporary).** Drove forklifts …

This will show the prospective employer that you are willing to work and be productive and supportive.

As you can see, the resume is quickly read to determine the experiences and skills you have acquired. The employer also looks for advancement within the company. Several sample resumes are following this section.

Note that the left margin provides space for notations by the interviewer. Another reason for the resume and application to have the same dates and information. (see applications)

What if there are gaps in the employment? They could be lay-offs or an incarceration. These should be left off the resume and addressed on cover letter or at the interview (particularly the incarceration). Since most companies will follow-up with previous employers, it is better to be upfront rather than be caught later.

The last part of your resume is education. This is expressed as name of school and location. If you served in the military, list the branch and courses of study. Your high school should be listed or if you received your GED in the military or other institutions, so state, ie: GED, U. S. Army.

EDUCATION: University of Kentucky, Bachelor of Arts, Business Administration, Lexington, Kentucky; U. S. Navy, Yeoman Class A School; Winchester High School, Winchester, Kentucky.

Education is to be placed after the experience, unless there are many degrees, technical degrees and fields of study, which supports your objective. If this is the case, place the education after your objective.

Having put all this information together, check the spelling and check it again. *Do not abbreviate!*

One page resume is ideal – do not run over two pages.

If the resume is two pages, do not staple. Be sure to add your name and page number to the second page – right side preferred:

JANE or JOHN DOE
Resume – Page Two

Use short sentences: Drove forklift; Operated Brake Machines; Operated CNC Milling Machines; Operated Production and Conveyor Equipment; Performed Scheduled Maintenance; Read Blueprints and Schematics; Laid-Out and Made Tool & Dies; Managed and Directed Accounting Department. Remember – you manage things - you direct and supervise people.

When mailing, use a 9"x12" envelope. Do not fold, as the Human Resources Department may want to scan your resume into their computer.

If sending your resume and cover letter by email, follow-up by regular mail and confirm that it was received.

JANE or JOHN DOE
123 Main Street
AnyTown, AnyState AnyZip
000-000-0000
email@abc.com

OBJECTIVE: To interview for the position in **Accounting**.

EXPERIENCE:

Jan 00 to
Present

ABC Corporation, Indianapolis, Indiana.
ACCOUNTING SUPERVISOR. Direct and coordinate activities of personnel engaged in calculating, posting, verifying and reconciling accounting records and reports. Monitor recordation of financial data for use in maintaining accounting and statistical records. Supervise and train personnel.

Sep 95 to
Jan 00

XYZ Corporation, Indianapolis, Indiana.
BOOKKEEPER. Verified, allocated and posted details of business transactions to subsidiary accounts in journals and computer files from documents. Summarized details. Compiled reports regarding cash receipts and expenditures, accounts payable and receivables, and profit and loss. Calculated employee wages. Prepared withholding taxes.

ACCOUNTING CLERK. Posted and verified financial data and maintained accounting records. Compiled and sorted invoices and checks. Verified and posted accounts receivables and payables. Operated calculators and computers.

EDUCATION: IUPUI, Accounting Major, Indianapolis, Indiana; Harrison Business College, Accounting Certificate, Indianapolis, Indiana; Graduate Arsenal Technical High School, Indianapolis, Indiana.

JANE or JOHN DOE (College Student)
123 Main Street
AnyTown, AnyState AnyZip
000-000-0000
email@abc.com

OBJECTIVE: To interview for the position in **Accounting**.

EDUCATION: Ball State University, Honor's College, Bachelors of Science, Accounting Major, Muncie, Indiana; U. S. Navy, Yeoman Class A School; Graduate North Decatur High School, Greensburg, Indiana;

EXPERIENCE:

May 06 to Aug 06	Fifth Third Bank, Indianapolis, Indiana. **ACCOUNTING INTERN (Summer Employment).** Developed annual income forecasts and monitored results. Researched and reported variances. Made presentations and recommendations to corporate management. Reconciled and reviewed general ledger accounts. Developed reports for Federal Reserve. Posted and examined journal entries in computer systems.
May 05 to Aug 05	Fifth Third Bank, Muncie, Indiana. **BANK TELLER (Summer Employment).** Managed bank accounts for commercial customers. Summarized customer complaints/questions and presented to management. Balanced cash drawer.
Dec 04 to Apr 05	Ball State University, Muncie, Indiana. **ACCOUNTING ASSISTANT.** Managed bike rental stands for Ball State University. Invoiced, set-up and maintained accounting records. Directed and trained personnel in computer skills.

8

JANE or JOHN DOE
123 Main Street
AnyTown, AnyState AnyZip
000-000-0000
email@abc.com

OBJECTIVE:	To interview for **Apprentice Electrician.**

EXPERIENCE:

Aug 01 to
Present

Infinity Sales & Service, Indianapolis, Indiana.
ASSISTANT SERVICE DIRECTOR. Interface with customers to consult and determine problems with vehicles. Recommend service actions and calculate costs. Communicate and dispatch repair work to service technicians. Furnish service background for customers and agency through computers. Assist in selling accessories. Monitor quality. Perform service management duties in absence of manager. Supervise and direct service technicians.

SERVICE CONSULTANT. Interface with customers to determine and resolve problems. Calculate costs. Trained service consultants in quality assurance and computer network operations.

SERVICE PORTER. Detailed vehicles – interior, exterior and engines. Maintained cleanliness of work area. Ran errands and purchased needed supplies.

Oct 00 to
Aug 01

Nissan Sales and Service, Indianapolis, Indiana.
DETAILER. Provided quality detailing of vehicles for three dealerships. Maintained inventory of needed supplies. Wrote and submitted purchase orders.

EDUCATION: Graduate Broad Ripple High School, Indianapolis, Indiana; ITT Technical Institute, Electronics and Engineering, Indianapolis, Indiana; Infiniti Central Region Training Programs: Client Management Skills; Service Skills; Selling Service and Enhancing Dealership Profitability, Chicago, Illinois; Larry Edwards & Associates, Skills Development and Improvement, Dallas, Texas.

JANE or JOHN DOE
123 Main Street
AnyTown, AnyState AnyZip
000-000-0000
email@abc.com

OBJECTIVE: To interview for the position of **APPRENTICE PLUMBER.**

EXPERIENCE: Pilkington, Inc., Shelbyville, Indiana.
PRODUCTION TEAM MEMBER. Received windshields and inspect for quality. Solder braid or metal clips onto windshields. Inspect and test for proper specifications. Pack into finish goods rack.

MACHINE OPERATOR. Load truck windshields onto carousal and conveyor in which an automated machine applies spacers and foam. Inspect product prior to and after manufacturing process.

SHIPPING CLERK. Organized and staged material for shipping. Operated forklift to load and unload tractor-trailers. Operated computer to input and print bills of lading. Verified in-house paperwork for quality and accuracy.

STORE ROOM CLERK. Issued operating materials and supplies to production members. Managed requisitions for items dispersed. Verified stock items and input into computer. Inventoried material and supplies.

EDUCATION: Graduate Morristown High School, Morristown, Indiana; Clarklift, Inc., Forklift Training and Certification, Shelbyville, Indiana.

NOTE: For those who have been incarcerated, do not show the dates of employment. Address those questions at the interview.

JANE or JOHN DOE (High School Student)
Living with Mom & Dad
Anytown, Anycity AnyZip
000-000-0000
email@abc.com

OBJECTIVE: To interview for **Production Work / Assembler.**

EXPERIENCE:

Jun 06 to   Quad Lynn Farms, Greensburg, Indiana
Aug 06   **Detasseling Crew Leader.** Called and scheduled crew for
                   detasseling seed corn. Prepared and drove detasseling
                   machinery. Trained and supervised crew in safety and
                   production.

                   Detasseling Crew Worker. Detasseled seed corn. Pulled
                   weeds from corn rolls.

                   Concession Stand (Summer Softball Leagues). Ordered
                   and replenished supplies – sandwiches, soda, candy, etc.
                   Prepared food. Maintained cleanliness. Closed concession
                   stand.

Jun 05 to   McDonalds, Batesville, Indiana.
Sep 05   **Cashier.** Received food orders and money from customers.
                   Assisted with other duties as directed. Maintained cleanliness,
                   courtesy and a pleasant atmosphere.

EDUCATION: Graduating from South Decatur High School in August 2007,
                   Greensburg, Indiana.

JANE or JOHN DOE
123 Main Street
AnyTown, AnyState AnyZip
000-000-0000
email@abc.com

OBJECTIVE: To interview for the position of **CARPENTER.**

EXPERIENCE:

Apr 00 to
Present

ABC Construction Company, Cincinnati, Ohio
CARPENTER. Construct new homes using carpenter's handtools and power tools, and conforming to local building codes. Study blueprints, sketches and building plans for information pertaining to type of material required. Prepare layout using rule, framing square and calipers. Assembles cut and shaped materials and fasten with nails, dowel pins or glue. Verify trueness. Build stairs. Erect framework and subflooring. Construct forms for concrete.

Jun 95 to
Apr 00

XYZ Construction, Indianapolis, Indiana.
CARPENTER APPRENTICE. Built rough wooden structures, such as concrete forms according to sketches, blueprints or oral instructions. Used handtools, power tools, and measuring instruments. Examined specifications to determine dimensions of structure. Measured boards and timbers and saw to required lengths. Braced forms in place. Lay tie rods. Installed door and window bucks. Attended building trades school weekly for the apprenticeship program.

Jan 93 to
Apr 00

BCD Fast Food, Rushville, Indiana.
COOK (Part Time). Received orders and cooked hamburgers and deep-fry french fries.   Took orders and worked cash register when needed. Maintained cleanliness.

EDUCATION: Graduate North Decatur High School, Greensburg, Indiana.

JANE or JOHN DOE
123 Main Street
AnyTown, AnyState AnyZip
000-000-0000
email@abc.com

OBJECTIVE: To interview for the position of **CHEF.**

EDUCATION: U. S. Marine Corps Culinary School; Florida Career Institute, Computer Network Technology, Lakeland, Florida; Indiana University, Psychology Major, Bloomington, Indiana.

EXPERIENCE:

Mi Amigos Restaurant, Indianapolis, Indiana.
MANAGER. Managed dine-in restaurant to prepare and serve consistently high quality foods in a clean environment. Directed, supervised and trained personnel. Prepared work schedules and payroll. Prepared menus. Purchased and inventoried necessary operating supplies, foods and equipment. Monitored maintenance of equipment. Managed interior and exterior cleanliness of property.

Szabo Food Services, Indianapolis, Indiana.
MAINTENANCE TECHNICIAN. Installed, maintained and repaired vending machines. Inventoried and replenished with products when necessary. Ordered necessary parts and consumable items for machines. Performed preventative maintenance. Collected and deposited monies.

NOTE: For those who have been incarcerated, do not show the dates of employment. Address those questions at the interview.

JANE or JOHN DOE
123 Main Street
AnyTown, AnyState AnyZip
000-000-0000
email@abc.com

OBJECTIVE: To interview for the position of **Chief Financial Officer.**

EXPERIENCE:

Jan 05 to
Present

Namera International Group, Indianapolis, Indiana.
CONTROLLER.   Report to President and Chief Financial
Officer of medium sized insurance holding company. Group
consists of five property casualty insurance companies that
market primarily nonstandard automotive and crop / hail
insurance. Managed all financial reporting and analysis of
non-standard automotive operation, systems development,
reinsurance coordination, actuarial reviews, and financial
regulatory compliance. Directed the development of
accounting and reinsurance system modules to integrate
with the premium and claim modules in network based
operating systems being developed. Coordinated annual and
quarterly actuarial and external audit reviews. Developed
and maintained relations with regulatory authorities.
Conducted accounting functions between newly acquired
affiliates and corporate headquarters. Assisted in the
accumulation and development of financial information for S-1
filing. Coordinated reinsurance programs for nonstandard
automotive operations. Assisted Corporate Counsel in
development of regulatory affairs and procedures.

Aug 03 to
Dec 05

Star Insurance Group, Chicago, Illinois.
CHIEF FINANCIAL OFFICER. Report to President and Chief
Operating Officer of an Insurance holding company, consisting
of four nonstandard automotive insurance companies.
Managed all financial aspects of the insurance operations.
Prepared, presented and interpreted quarterly financial data
and developed the first formal financial plan to the Board
of Directors. Developed and maintained relationships with
consulting actuaries and various regulatory authorities.
Analyzed and updated reinsurance programs to comply with
businesses being marketed. Directed the

14

Implementation of a mechanized general ledger and accounts payable system that resulted in the reduction in costs and an increase in monthly reporting efficiencies.

Jan 01 to
Nov 05

McIntosh and Associates, Libertyville, Illinois
PRESIDENT. Specialized in litigation support, reinsurance audits and organizational realignment. Reconstructed reinsurance transactions for a former syndicate on the Illinois Insurance Exchange. Assisted in litigation support related to reinsurance, reserve analysis, compliance and audit negligence resulting in the successful termination of all litigation. Participated in a regulatory financial and operation review of service carriers for the New Jersey Joint Underwriting Association that resulted in the implementation of additional underwriting and claim cost controls.

Jan 99 to
Dec 00

Risk Management Corporation, New York, New York.
CONSULTANT / ADMINISTRATOR. A privately held litigation support, forensic accounting and third party administrator. Established Midwestern office with staffing to serve as administrator for client's individual health business, including the reconstruction of the field force, production efforts, underwriting and claims. Managed the reconstruction of reinsurance treaties and related transactions of a liquidated multi-line company on behalf of a state insurance department to support litigation.

EDUCATION:

Graduate Quincy College, Bachelor of Science, Accounting, Quincy, Illinois; Member Insurance Accounting and Statistical Association.

JANE or JOHN DOE
123 Main Street
AnyTown, AnyState AnyZip
000-000-0000
email@abc.com

OBJECTIVE: To interview for the position of **Construction Inspector.**

EDUCATION: Columbus Vocational School, Industrial Electricity; Purdue School of Technology, Organizational Management, Columbus, Indiana; Graduate Connersville High School, Connersville, Indiana.

EXPERIENCE:

Jun 02 to
Present

Ace Construction, Columbus, Indiana.
CONSTRUCTION FOREMAN. Managed construction projects. Direct, train and supervise construction personnel. Coordinate and schedule sub-contractors, acquire necessary materials and monitor progress in the building of commercial and industrial buildings. Study and follow local codes and regulations. Read blueprints, schematics and monitor quality. Operate heavy equipment when necessary.

Apr 95 to
May 02

Baker Concrete, Columbus, Ohio.
CONSTRUCTION FOREMAN. Managed the construction of commercial buildings. Laid-out building locations and excavated foundations and slab sites. Installed rebar and manufactured forms. Calculated the amount of concrete to be poured. Acquired the necessary equipment. Directed the pouring and finishing of concrete. Trained and supervised personnel. Read blueprints, schematics and operated electronic and mechanical measuring instruments.

Aug 93 to
Apr 95

Ace Construction, Columbus, Indiana.
JOURNEYMAN CARPENTER. Installed forms, rebars and supervised the pouring and finishing of concrete. Trained and supervised apprentices. Read blueprints and operated measuring instruments. Operated heavy equipment.

May 93 to
Aug 93

Dayton Construction, Indianapolis, Indiana.
LEAD CARPENTER (Temporary). Assisted with the construction of a hospital.

JANE or JOHN DOE
123 Main Street
AnyTown, AnyState AnyZip
000-000-0000
email@abc.com

OBJECTIVE: To interview for the position in **Electronics.**

EDUCATION: Gary Area Career Center, Electronics Technology, Gary
Indiana; U. S. Air Force Basic, Intermediate and Advanced
Electronics School; U. S. Air Force Photographic Systems
School; U. S. Air Force Leadership School; and, Graduate
Gary West Side High School, Gary, Indiana.

EXPERIENCE:

Jan 86 to   U. S. Air Force.
Present   **JOURNEYMAN AVIONIC SENSOR TECHNICIAN.**
Inspected, installed, maintained and repaired avionics
sensor equipment, such as: Infrared receivers, lasers,
transmitters, and radar control systems. Managed tool
crib. Operated computer controlled test stations. Assisted
in the development, implementation and management of a
hazardous waste management program. Directed and trained
electron maintenance personnel.

AVIONIC ELECTRONIC SYSTEMS TECHNICIAN. Installed
repaired and maintained aircraft video systems. Tested
and replaced components. Conducted major modifications
for manufacturers' retrofits. Fabricated wiring harnesses.
Monitored installations. Installed, monitored and serviced
experimental video and laser systems. Read schematics,
specifications and blueprints.

AEROSPACE PHOTOGRAPHIC SYSTEMS TECHNICIAN.
Installed, maintained and repaired radar and video systems.
Operated electronic test and diagnostic equipment. Calibrated
test and diagnostic instruments and equipment. Interpreted
wiring and schematic diagrams. Conducted avionics systems
safety inspections to include: Cockpit instruments, wiring,
radar and weapon delivery systems.

JANE or JOHN DOE
123 Main Street
AnyTown, AnyState AnyZip
000-000-0000
email@abc.com

OBJECTIVE: To interview for the position of **Electronics Mechanic.**

EDUCATION: Ball State University, General Studies, Muncie, Indiana;
U. S. Air Force Fundamental, Basic and Advanced Electronics
School; U. S. Air Force Radar Testing School; Gardner Denver
Wire Wrap Technician School, Grand Haven, Michigan;
Graduate Greenfield High School, Greenfield, Indiana.

EXPERIENCE:

Jul 85 to
Jan 07

Naval Air Warfare Center, Indianapolis, Indiana
ELECTRONIC MECHANIC. Managed the maintenance
and repair of automated machinery. Read schematics,
specifications and prints. Operated automated equipment to
hard-wire subassemblies and final configurations. Monitored
operation of equipment including scheduled maintenance.
Directed and trained personnel on the safe operation of
equipment. Maintained critical parts inventory.

ELECTRONIC MECHANIC / QUALITY CONTROL. Tested
discrete levels of wiring configurations. Final testing of
products to military specifications. Performed destructive
testing to obtain quantitative measurements for statistical
process control charts. Inspected assemblies for proper and
correct wiring, wire dress and wire layout.

ELECTRONIC ASSEMBLER. Assembled components into
printed wiring boards, installed wiring harnesses and installed
completed boards into final configuration per schematics,
blueprints and specifications.

JANE or JOHN DOE
123 Main Street
AnyTown, AnyState AnyZip
000-000-0000
email@abc.com

OBJECTIVE: Interview for the position of **Hazardous Waste Specialist.**

EDUCATION: U. S. Naval Officers Advanced Environmental Management
School; U. S. Naval Officers Environmental Law School;
U. S. Naval Officers Environmental Negotiation School;
U. S. Marine Corps Advanced Hazardous Materials / Waste
School; Department of Transportation Advanced Hazardous
Material / Waste Transportation School; U. S. Marine
Corps Shelf-Life Management School; U. S. Marine Corps
Hazardous Waste Emergency Response School; U. S. Naval
Maritime Spill Response School; U. S. Marine Corps NCO
Executive Leadership / Management School; Graduate
Arlington High School, Indianapolis, Indiana.

Dec 80 to   U. S. Marine Corps.
Jan 07   **ASSISTANT HAZARDOUS MATERIAL/WASTE MANAGER**
Assisted with planning, budgeting, organizing, directing,
controlling and coordinating the operations of a hazardous
waste facility. Conducted studies on waste management
projects and provided recommendations on treatment and
containment of hazardous waste. Participated in developing
hazardous waste policies and procedures. Assessed waste
treatment and disposal alternatives. Developed cost scenarios
on alternative methods of disposal and documented benefits.
Provided technical assistance and training for hazardous
waste spills.

ENVIRONMENTAL INSPECTOR / INSTRUCTOR MANAGER
Managed environmental auditing department to monitor and
direct compliance. Managed and monitored the compliance
of 224 sites in accordance with state and federal regulations.
Generated quarterly reports of audit findings.

JANE or JOHN DOE
123 Main Street
AnyTown, AnyState AnyZip
000-000-0000
email@abc.com

OBJECTIVE: Interview for the position of **Heavy Equipment Operator.**

EXPERIENCE:

May 01 to
Present

ABC Company, Indianapolis, Indiana.
HEAVY EQUIPMENT OPERATOR. Operate backhoes, excavators, dozers, front-end loaders, trenchers and cranes to move earth for commercial, residential and industrial construction. Perform preventative maintenance. Set forms and finish concrete. Use lasers to calculate grades for construction. Read blueprints and layouts. Interface with building inspectors for approvals.

Jul 00 to
May 01

XYZ Construction, Indianapolis, Indiana.
HEAVY EQUIPMENT OPERATOR. Operated heavy equipment to move earth and lay pipe. Read blueprints, specificaction sheets and layouts. Interfaced with construction inspectors for necessary approvals. Maintained equipment.

May 99 to
Jul 00

R & R Construction, Franklin, Indiana.
HEAVY EQUIPMENT OPERATOR. Operated heavy construction equipment to dig and lay gas lines. Read blueprints and specifications sheets. Installed meters and gas lines into new commercial, industrial and residential construction.

EDUCATION: Graduate New Palestine High School, New Palestine, Indiana; Graduate Blue River Vocational Technical School, Automotive Mechanics, Shelbyville, Indiana; and U. S. Army National Guard, Aircraft Sheet Metal Fabricating School.

JANE or JOHN DOE
123 Main Street
AnyTown, AnyState AnyZip
000-000-0000
email@abc.com

OBJECTIVE: To interview for the position of **Help Desk Coordinator.**

EDUCATION: Indiana University, Bachelor of Science, Business Administration, Indianapolis, Indiana; Marian College, Business Administration Major, Indianapolis, Indiana; U. S. Navy Storekeeper School; and, Graduate Cathedral High School, Indianapolis, Indiana.

EXPERIENCE:

Sep 05 to
Present

Bell Industries, Indianapolis, Indiana.
HELP DESK SUPPORT SPECIALIST. Assist users with operational (hardware and software) problems. Maintained recorded problems and made recommendations to technicians for resolutions. Installed and up-dated software. Change passwords, answer questions regarding software, instruct users on e-mail software packages, and solve peripheral equipment problems.

Aug 02 to
Sep 05

Manpower Technical Services, Indianapolis, Indiana.
HELP DESK SUPPORT SPECIALIST (Temporary). Assisted health care professionals with the operation of network and software packages. Resolved problems in operational procedures. Made recommendations for hardware and software purchases. Set-up equipment and installed software. Trained personnel on network use.

Jul 00 to
Jul 02

Computers Today, Indianapolis, Indiana.
SALES ASSOCIATE. Sold computer equipment, software and supplies through catalog operations to industrial, commercial, government and private individuals. Prepared and monitored bids.

JANE or JOHN DOE
123 Main Street
AnyTown, AnyState AnyZip
000-000-0000
email@abc.com

OBJECTIVE: To interview for the position of **HEATING AND AIR CONDITIONING INSTALLER-SERVICER.**

EXPERIENCE:

Sep 04 to
Present

Herbert's HVAC, Inc., Connersville, Indiana.
SHEET METAL WORKER. Assist with the fabrication and installation of heating and air conditioning ductwork. Read and interpret blueprints, sketches and product specifications to determine sequence and methods of fabricating, assembling and installing sheet metal ductwork. Operate shears, brakes, presses, and forming rolls. Weld, solder, bolt, screw, clip, caulk or bonds component parts to assemble products. Use measuring instruments, such as, calipers, dial indicators, gauges and micrometers. Operated computer-aided-drafting equipment.

Jan 02 to
Aug 04

Stahle's Hardware, Greensburg, Indiana.
GAS APPLIANCE-SERVICER. Installed, tested, adjusted and repaired regulators, ranges, and heater in customer's homes. Measured, cut, thread and connect pipe to feeder line and installed appliance, using cutters, threaders and wrenches. Dismantle appliances and replace defective pipes, thermocouples, thermostats, valves and spindles.

EDUCATION: Ivy Tech Heating and Air Conditioning Technical School, Columbus, Indiana. Graduate North Central High School, Columbus, Indiana.

JANE or JOHN DOE
123 Main Street
AnyTown, AnyState AnyZip
000-000-0000
email@abc.com

OBJECTIVE: To interview for the position of **ILLUSTRATOR.**

EDUCATION: Bachelors Degree, Marian College, English Major,
Indianapolis, Indiana; Graduate Shelbyville High School,
Shelbyville, Indiana.

EXPERIENCE:

Aug 98 to   KL Corporation, Shelbyville, Indiana.
Present   **SENIOR ARTIST.** Create and design artwork for advertising
illustrations. Color separate graphics using computer
programs. Monitor artwork process. Communicate
with marketing and sales personnel to meet customer's
requirements. Coordinate with production to monitor product
quality. Manage department. Train and direct personnel.

JUNIOR ARTIST. Produced and maintained quality control
of newly designed graphics and graphic changes. Mixed
photographic chemicals accurately for film development.
Set-up and use electronic measuring instruments. Produce
precision positioning of printed line artwork.

PRINTING PLATE MAKER. Produced and monitored
quality of printing plates. Produced step and repeat precision
negatives.

COMPUTER
SKILLS: Macromedia Freehand 8.0; Adobe Photoshop 5.0; Streamline
2.0; Adobe Type Manager Deluxe; Conversion File Navigator;
Macromedia Flash 2.

JANE or JOHN DOE
123 Main Street
AnyTown, AnyState AnyZip
000-000-0000
email@abc.com

OBJECTIVE: To interview for the position of **IRON WORKER.**

EXPERIENCE:

Mar 05 to Present

Baker Steel Works, Madison, Indiana.
METAL BUILDING ASSEMBLER. Assemble prefabricated metal building according to blueprint specifications, using hand tools, power tools, and hoisting equipment. Use hoist to erect frames of building. Bolt steel frame members together. Bolt sheet metal panels and insulation materials to framework. Read blueprints to install doors, windows, and skylights. Use cutting torch.

Jan 02 to Mar 05

Hayes Farms, North Vernon, Indiana.
FARM EQUIPMENT MECHANIC. Service and make minor repairs to farm tractors, trucks, harvesters, and combines using hard tools. Observe and examine machinery and parts in operation to detect malfunctions or defective units. Replace components. Adjust timing of motors, lubricate, wash, paint and clean vehicles and attachments. Assist other workers in more complex maintenance tasks, such as overhaul of machinery, erection of buildings and structures. Repaired plumbing. Operated welders.

EDUCATION: Ivy Tech Mechanical School, Indianapolis, Indiana; Graduate South Decatur High School, Greensburg, Indiana.

JANE or JOHN DOE
123 Main Street
AnyTown, AnyState AnyZip
000-000-0000
email@abc.com

OBJECTIVE:	To interview for a **Manufacturing Machine Operator.**
EXPERIENCE:	
Oct 05 to Present	ABC Company, Vincennes, Indiana. **MACHINE OPERATOR / MAINTENANCE ASSISTANT.** Set-up and operate drill, punch and brake presses. Set-up and operate resistance, MIG and TIG welders. Coordinate and stage material from manufacturing and warehouse to production. Operate forklift.
Aug 01 to Sep 05	Vincennes University, Vincennes, Indiana. **METALWORKING TECHNOLOGY (Student).** Studied theory and machining practices to produce industrial goods in a machine shop environment. Performed measurements, layouts and inspections, machine tool processes and operations, metallurgy, shop math and blueprint reading. Operated CNC lathes, drill presses, milling machines, precision grinders, metal saws, and mechanical / digital measuring instruments. Produced prototype parts to one ten-thousandth inch.
Aug 97 to Aug 01	U. S. Marine Corps. **U. S. PRESIDENTIAL SUPPORT TECHNICIAN.** Provided security for U. S. President and presidential helicopter. Directed and trained Marines in proper procedures in security and ceremonies. Planned and scheduled duty hours. Inventoried and requisitioned security supplies. Inspected personnel. Maintained daily work journals.
EDUCATION:	Graduate Vincennes University, Metalworking Technology, Vincennes, Indiana; U. S. Marine Corps Combat Training School; U. S. Marine Military Police Academy; Northern Virginia Community College, Engineering Major, Sterling, Virginia; Graduate Arsenal Technical High School, Indianapolis, Indiana

JANE or JOHN DOE
123 Main Street
AnyTown, AnyState AnyZip
000-000-0000
email@abc.com

OBJECTIVE: To interview for the position of **Maintenance Mechanic.**

EDUCATION: U. S. Navy Aviation Fundamental School; U. S. Navy
Hydraulics Theory School; U. S. Navy Hydraulics Component
Test School; and U. S. Navy Hydraulic Component and
Operations (pumps, servos and actuators) School; Graduate
Thomas Carr Howe High School, Indianapolis, Indiana.

EXPERIENCE:

Jan 95 to   ABC Company, Inc., Indianapolis, Indiana.
Present   **JOURNEYMAN MILLWRIGHT.** Install, maintain and repair
production machines and electric motors. Order repair parts
and maintain critical inventory. Fabricate operational parts.
Use mechanical measuring devices and instruments. Operate
welding equipment – MIG, TIG and Arc. Maintain and repair
hydraulic and pneumatic systems. Train apprentices.

MILLWRIGHT APPRENTICE. Installed, repaired and
performed preventative maintenance on heavy production
equipment. Obtained certification on cranes, scissor lifts,
and forklift operating. Maintained hydraulic and pneumatic
systems. Installed and repaired conveyors. Removed and
built concrete foundations for equipment installations.

MAINTENANCE MECHANIC / MILLWRIGHT HELPER.
Installed, maintained and repaired production equipment. Built
concrete foundations for new machine installations. Operated
airless paint sprayers. Welded. Installed and repaired
equipment plumbing. Operated forklifts.

JANE or JOHN DOE
123 Main Street
AnyTown, AnyState AnyZip
000-000-0000
email@abc.com

OBJECTIVE: To interview for **PHYSICAL THERAPIST ASSISTANT.**

EDUCATION: Associates Degree, Physical Therapist, University of Indianapolis; Blue River Career Center, Health Career Certification, Shelbyville, Indiana; Graduate Morristown High School, Morristown, Indiana.

CLINICAL ROTATIONS: St. Mary's Medical Center, Inpatient General Acute Population, Evansville, Indiana; St. Francis Hospital Outpatient Sports Medicine, Indianapolis, Indiana; and, Reid Hospital, Pediatric Population, Richmond, Indiana.

EXPERIENCE:

Jun 05 to Present — Rehabilitation Hospital of Indiana, Indianapolis. **THERAPY TECHNICIAN.** Assist physical therapist with treatment sessions and procedures. Transport patients within hospital. Research and order equipment and supplies. Maintain inventories. Perform data entry of patient information. Maintain cleanliness of treatment area.

Apr 05 to Jun 05 — Nippisun, Shelbyville, Indiana **QUALITY CONTROL SPECIALIST (Summer).** Inspected and tested quality of raw plastic material. Charted and documented results of tests.

Apr 04 to Apr 05 — Nova Care at Lockfield Village, Indianapolis, Indiana. **REHABILITATION TECHNICIAN.** Assisted therapists with treatment sessions. Set-up and prepared sterile field for wound care. Cleaned, prepared and repaired rehab equipment. Performed data entry and general office duties.

JANE or JOHN DOE
123 Main Street
AnyTown, AnyState AnyZip
000-000-0000
email@abc.com

OBJECTIVE: To interview for the position of **Plumber.**

EXPERIENCE:

Jun 98 to
Present

ABC Mechanical Services, Greensburg, Indiana.
PLUMBER / PIPEFITTER. Assemble, install, and repair pipes, fittings, and fixtures of heating, water and drainage systems in industrial and residential establishments, according to specifications and plumbing codes. Study building plans and working drawings. Use hand tools and power tools. Cut, thread and bend pipes to specifications. Assemble and install valves and fittings. Assist with the installation of air conditioning units. Weld holding fixtures to steel structures. Install commercial fixtures – water heaters, softeners, kitchen appliances, and refrigeration units. Perform preventative maintenance.

May 97 to
Aug 97

DEF Dairy Farms, Shelbyville, Indiana.
MAINTENANCE WORKER. Assisted with the maintenance of milking machines. Pump milk from receptacles into storage tanks. Clean and sterilize equipment. Assisted with the maintenance of farm equipment.

EDUCATION: Graduate St. Paul High School, St. Paul, Indiana. IvyTech Building Trades School for Plumbing, Columbus, Indiana.

JANE or JOHN DOE
123 Main Street
AnyTown, AnyState AnyZip
000-000-0000
email@abc.com

OBJECTIVE: To interview for **PRODUCTION COORDINATOR.**

EXPERIENCE:

Apr 97 to
Present

Delta Faucet, Greensburg, Indiana.
MATERIAL HANDLER. Read work orders, pick raw material from warehouse and deliver to manufacturing and production. Operate forklifts to deliver and return stock. Maintain inventory via bar coding. Enter data into computer for production.

STORE CLERK. Coordinated and directed the flow of warehouse material to handlers. Prepared orders and monitored inventory. Operated computer and performed general office work.

TOOL CRIB ATTENDANT. Ordered, inventoried and issued manufacturing tools. Read blueprints, working drawings and used precision measuring devices. Operated computer to maintain accountability. Maintained inventory of production machine parts and supplies.

BRAZING OPERATOR. Operated automated cleaning systems to clean and flux copper parts. Brazed parts, performed quality inspections and packaged for shipment. Read specifications and operated precision measuring instruments.

EDUCATION: Delta Faucet, OSHA Forklift Certification, HazMat Certification, and Respirator Certification, Greensburg, Indiana; Greensburg High School, Qualified Medication Aide, Greensburg, Indiana.

JANE or JOHN DOE
123 Main Street
AnyTown, AnyState AnyZip
000-000-0000
email@abc.com

OBJECTIVE: To interview for a position in **QUALITY ASSURANCE.**

EXPERIENCE:

May 04 to
Present

Libbey-Owens-Ford Corporation, Shelbyville, Indiana.
SCREEN FABRICATOR. Fabricate and process screens for automotive glass production. Manage night shift and direct personnel in trouble-shooting and firing of glass. Monitor specifications to blend paints and silver pastes to specified firing temperatures. Maintain inventory and reports. Use Statistical Process Control (SPC) and measuring instruments to control variation of inventory and final products. Operate computer.

Aug 02 to
May 04

GECOM Corporation, Greensburg, Indiana.
PRODUCTION WORKER. Assembled automotive door latches. Inspected, packaged and staged finished products for domestic shipments.

EDUCATION: Indiana University Purdue University at Indianapolis and Columbus, Indiana, Physical Therapy Major; Graduate North Decatur High School, Greensburg, Indiana.

ACTIVITIES and
HONORS:

Alpha Sigma Lambda, IUPUI, Indianapolis, Indiana; Deans List, IUPUI, Indianapolis, Indiana; Libbey-Owns-Ford, Total Quality Management Award, Shelbyville, Indiana.

JANE or JOHN DOE
123 Main Street
AnyTown, AnyState AnyZip
000-000-0000
email@abc.com

OBJECTIVE:	To interview for the position in **Sales.**

EXPERIENCE:

Jan 00 to Present	RST Representatives, Indianapolis, Indiana. **MANUFACTURERS' REPRESENTATIVE.** Sell multiple manufactured products to wholesalers on commission basis within central United States. Demonstrate and sell features, advantages and benefits. Write proposals and bids. Close. Arrange for installations. Sell service and preventative maintenance agreements.
Sep 94 to Dec 99	GHI Corporation, Columbus, Indiana. **SALES REPRESENTATIVE, INDUSTRIAL MACHINERY.** Sold metal working equipment utilizing knowledge of manufacturing and production. Reviewed existing plant machinery layout and made recommendations for new installations. Demonstrated and proposed new equipment.
Aug 90 to Sep 94	ABC Company, Columbus, Indiana. **SALESMAN, BUILDING EQUIPMENT / SUPPLIES.** Sold building materials, equipment and supplies to include heating and air-conditioning equipment, insulation, glass, floor tiles, brick, lumber, etc. Made recommendations regarding equipment and construction methods.
EDUCATION:	IvyTech, Business Management, Columbus, Indiana; Cleveland Machinery Corporation, Sales and Maintenance School, Cleveland, Ohio; U. S. Navy Pipefitters School; Graduate, Columbus East High School, Columbus, Indiana.

JANE or JOHN DOE
123 Main Street
AnyTown, AnyState AnyZip
000-000-0000
email@abc.com

OBJECTIVE: To interview for the position of **Secretary/Receptionist**.

EXPERIENCE:

Apr 00 to
Present

Department of Workforce Development, Indianapolis, Indiana.
SECRETARY. Schedule appointments. Relieve manager
of clerical work, minor administrative and business details.
Read and route incoming correspondence. Compose and
type routine correspondence. File correspondence and other
records. Answer telephones, provide information and route
callers to appropriate departments. Greet visitors.

DATA ENTRY CLERK. Operated keyboard to enter data
into computer. Entered alphabetic, numeric and symbolic
data from source documents. Operated word processing
equipment to compile, type, revise, combine, edit, print and
store documents.

Mar 98 to
Apr 00

XYZ Corporation, Indianapolis, Indiana.
RECEPTIONIST (Temporary). Greeted and received
customers to determine nature of business and direct them
to proper destination. Arranged appointments. Operated
multi-line telephone system. Typed memos, correspondence,
reports and other documents.

EDUCATION: Indiana Business College, Secretarial Courses, Indianapolis,
Indiana; IUPUI Continuing Studies, Word Processing School,
Indianapolis, Indiana; U. S. Navy Yeoman School; Graduate
Warren Central High School, Indianapolis, Indiana.

**COMPUTER
SKILLS:**   Microsoft Word; Windows XP, WordPerfect; Excel; Dbase;
Lotus AMI Pro; PowerPoint, and Harvard Graphics.

. JANE or JOHN DOE
123 Main Street
AnyTown, AnyState AnyZip
000-000-0000
email@abc.com

OBJECTIVE: To Interview for **Special Education, Title 1 Teacher.**

EDUCATION: University of Indianapolis, BS Elementary Education with Endorsement in Learning Disabilities; State University of West Georgia, M.Ed. Special Education, Carrollton, Georgia; State University of West Georgia, Ed.S. Special Education Administration, Carrollton, Georgia; Graduate Burney High School, Burney, Indiana.

EXPERIENCE:

Jul 03 to Present — Franklin County Educational Service Center, Columbus, Ohio. **PRE-SCHOOL SPECIAL NEEDS TEACHER.** Teaching in a certified pre-school program within a pubic elementary school.

Jul 91 to May 03 — Cartersville City School Board, Cartersville, Georgia. **PRIMARY SCHOOL TEACHER – TITLE 1.** Taught reading and math to first and second grades. Special Education resource teacher – interrelated disabilities.

Jul 91 to Jul 97 — Cartersville Housing Authority, Cartersville, Georgia. **GED INSTRUCTOR (Part-time).** Taught small groups of GED students twice weekly.

COMMITTEES: Co-Director of Before School Program; Pay for Performance Committee; Southern Association of Colleges and Schools (SACS); Mentor Committee; Parent / Community Involvement Committee Co-Chairperson; Leadership Committee; Special Education Team Leader; Student Support Teach Chairperson.

SKILLS TRAINING Orchard Plus Training; ClarisWorks Computer Training; IDEA Reauthorization; Educating Children Living in Poverty; Charter Schools Implementation; The Herrman Reading Method; Developing and Implementing School Renewal Plans; Sign Language; Hands on Science; and Community Based Instruction.

JANE or JOHN DOE
123 Main Street
AnyTown, AnyState AnyZip
000-000-0000
email@abc.com

OBJECTIVE: To interview for the position of **Tool & Die Maker.**

EXPERIENCE:

Apr 92 to
Present

AC Bearing, Inc., Batesville, Indiana.
JOURNEYWORKER TOOL & DIE MAKER. Read blueprints to determine material needs. Obtain material from tool room. Set-up shaper, mills, drill presses. Program and set-up CNC mills and grinders; program and set-up EDM machines; process and heat-treat materials. Precision grind. Read micrometers, calipers, mikes and precision instruments. Supervise and direct employees.

GROUP LEADER. Supervised, directed and trained personnel on blueprint reading, material requirements and monitor production output. Interfaced with engineering to solve production and die problems. Monitored safety.

TOOL GRINDER. Produced tooling in tool room. Read blueprints and specifications. Regrind tools to specifications. Used precision measuring instruments. Operated cutter-grinder, external and internal grinders, and center grinders.

CNC LATHE OPERATOR. Set-up, operated and monitored CNC Lathe. Made tool adjustments.

EDUCATION: Graduate Clarksburg High School, Clarksburg, Indiana; Sodick Enterprises, EDM Technical School, Chicago, Illinois; U. S. Army Heavy Armor School; U. S. Army Projectionist School.

JANE or JOHN DOE
123 Main Street
AnyTown, AnyState AnyZip
000-000-0000
email@abc.com

OBJECTIVE: To interview for the position of **Tractor-Trailer Truck Driver.**

EXPERIENCE:

May 02 to Present	ABC Trucking Company, Indianapolis, Indiana. **TRACTOR-TRAILER TRUCK DRIVER.** Transport products to companies in Indiana and surrounding states. Supervise loading and unloading. Maintain paperwork and bills of lading. Check invoices. Perform preventative maintenance on vehicle as required by DOT. Operate computer. CDL Class A license with endorsements.
Mar 02 to May 02	DEF Company, Indianapolis, Indiana. **REFRIGERATED VAN DRIVER (Temporary).** Deliver perishable produce to central states. Maintained paperwork as required by DOT. Inspected equipment and products. Operated computers. Maintained CDL Class A license with endorsements in good standing.
Jan 95 to Mar 02	OTR Company, Indianapolis, Indiana. **TRACTOR-TRAILER TRUCK DRIVER.** Delivered freight to west coast for assigned companies. Maintained paperwork. Routed loads. Directed and supervised loading. Operated forklift. Performed DOT inspections of tractor, trailer and loads. Maintained CDL Class A with endorsements.
Jan 93 to Jan 95	XYZ Trucking, Indianapolis, Indiana. **TRACTOR-TRAILER TRUCK DRIVER.** Assigned to XYZ Worldwide to pick-up and deliver high valued products. Drove from Indianapolis to Chicago O'Hare. Secured containers. Maintained paperwork and bills of lading.
EDUCATION:	West Virginia State College, Criminology Major, Dunbar, West Virginia; U. S. Air Force War College; and, U. S. Air Force Navigator Training School.

JANE or JOHN DOE
123 Main Street
AnyTown, AnyState AnyZip
000-000-0000
email@abc.com

OBJECTIVE: To interview for the position of **Vice President Finance.**

EDUCATION: Indiana University, Bachelors of Science, Business Administration and Finance, Indianapolis, Indiana; Bank One Management Training Seminars and Courses; and, U. S. Navy Aviation School.

EXPERIENCE:

Feb 02 to Present

Bankers Capital Funding Corporation, Indianapolis, Indiana. **VICE PRESIDENT and SERVICING MANAGER.** Manage all aspects of a multi-national commercial/multi-family mortgage-servicing department. Coordinate procedures to provide accurate detail for the remitting and reporting of investor funds. Direct and review the performance of all servicing staff.

LOAN ADMINISTRATION OFFICER. Managed daily servicing operations of commercial servicing department. Monitored servicing activities of various departments for proper administration and control. Created monthly departmental managerial financial status reports. Directed and trained servicing staff.

Jan 98 to Feb 02

Business National Bank, Indianapolis, Indiana. **COMMERCIAL AUDIT OFFICER.** Created and managed commercial audit department. Monitored all loans for compliance to credit policies. Served as liaison between company and senior loan committee. Prepared financial reports from disseminated information. Directed staff evaluations and training requirements.

Feb 96 to Jan 98

American State Bank, Chicago, Illinois. **SENIOR AUDIT EXAMINER.** Audited asset-based loans on Fortune 100 companies with loan balances in the multi-million dollar categories. Conducted on-site audit reviews. Proposed financing alternatives and recommendations.

36

JANE or JOHN DOE
123 Main Street
AnyTown, AnyState AnyZip
000-000-0000
email@abc.com

OBJECTIVE: To interview for the position in **Warehousing.**

EXPERIENCE:

Apr 04 to
Present

ABC Company, Indianapolis, Indiana.
DISTRIBUTION CENTER WORKER / SUPERVISOR.
Operate forklift truck to unload incoming freight. Check and
inspect products against purchase orders and bills of lading.
Input data into computer. Stage materials for warehouse.
Direct personnel in stocking merchandise. Maintain inventory.
Pick merchandise to fill orders. Operate wrapping machine.
Load trucks against load plans.

Mar 96 to
Apr 04

XYZ Company, Indianapolis, Indiana.
INVENTORY MANAGER. Inventoried existing stock and
placed production orders on manufacturing and purchasing
to replenish inventory. Released stock to production. Staged
finished products for shipping. Monitored delivery and
customer orders. Input data into computer. Operated forklifts.

SET-UP SUPERVISOR. Set-up daily shipping orders and
conveyors for production workers. Directed and trained
personnel in the assembly of products. Monitored production
flows and replenished product lines. Maintained paperwork.

PRODUCTION WORKER. Picked and packaged orders
from customer purchase orders. Operated conveyor system.
Maintained paperwork.

EDUCATION: U. S. Army Bradley Missile Training School; Graduate
Lawrence North High School, Indianapolis, Indiana.

Salary History

Some companies will want you to submit a salary history. They do this for several reasons:

1. Companies will increase wages to those who produce – they want to see if you fit into that group;

2. It gives them a negotiation edge when starting a new employee; and,

3. Based on the skills and experience, they can see where they need to place a prospective employee within their wage structure.

The salary history is quite simple and straight forward. On a separate page, format the below as it corresponds to your resume:

SALARY HISTORY (SAMPLES)

JANE or JOHN DOE
123 Main Street
AnyTown, AnyState AnyZip
000-000-0000
email@abc.com

COMPANY	POSITION	WAGES
XYZ Company	Controller	to $93,250
JKL Company	Chief Financial Officer	to $78,500
ABC Company	President	to $46.000

OR

COMPANY	POSITION	WAGES
ABC Company	DC Worker/Supervisor	to $15.00 hr
XYZ Company	Inventory Manager	to $12.50 hr
	Set-up Supervisor	$11.00 hr
	Production Worker	$10.00 hr

THE COVER LETTER

You have developed a resume which commun-
icates your skills, experiences and education.
You have a clear job objective. You have
been networking with your friends, family, and
organizations. You have been knocking on
prospective employers doors. If turned down by
a prospective employer, ask them if they know of
companies who are hiring. It works!

You know the job market is very competitive.
The companies continue to downsize. Some job
seekers are accepting positions at lower salaries.

Listed below is advice from over 4,000 hiring
managers:

> Be computer literate
> Network
> Update and learn new skills
> Research hiring companies
> Be persistent
> Target your market – no shotgun mailings

Now it's time to place a cover letter to your resume.
There are two types cover letters – the first one is
responding to an advertisement. The second is

sending a company your resume cold. Remember, 85% of all jobs are not advertised, posted, or made available to the general public. Remember – do not staple or fold your resume and cover letter.

If the company does not provide a contact and/ or company name to mail your resume and cover letter, simply address the cover letter as indicated below.

ABC Company (and/or the P. O. Box only)
P. O. Box 1234
Indianapolis, Indiana 12345

Machine Set-Up Operator:

In response to your need for a machine set-up operator, ...

Instead of Dear…, print the name of the position (in bold type) as listed in the newspaper. Then start with the text of your cover letter as listed above.

If you are responding to J. Jones (as listed in the ad) and don't know the gender of the person to whom you are sending your resume, it is proper to address your cover letter to: Dear J. Jones:.

If you are in a profession that requires writing research papers, it is to your advantage to enclose your curriculum vitae.

...

THE COVER LETTER (SAMPLE)

(Responding to an advertisement)

JANE or JOHN DOE
123 Main Street
AnyTown, AnyState AnyZip
000-000-0000
email@abc.com

Current Date

J. Jones
XYZ Corporation
123 Main Street
Anytown, Anystate 12345

Dear J. Jones:

In response to your need for a/an (enter the advertised job title), (state where the job was listed, ie: as listed in the *Indianapolis Star*), I would appreciate the opportunity to evaluate my background and qualifications with you. There is a match between the advertised requirements of the position and my experience, skills and education.

As a/an (enter the specific job title), I have the experience and knowledge to (list the requirements as printed in the advertisement). I am proficient in the use of (list those items which will provide added value). I can provide quality services to your requirements and contribute to the production, profitability, safety and success of your organization.

I welcome the opportunity to discuss any possibilities with you.

Sincerely,

Jane or John Doe

Enclosure: Resume

Answering an Ad for a Nondestructive Tester.

JANE or JOHN DOE
123 Main Street
AnyTown, AnyState AnyZip
000-000-0000
email@abc.com

Current Date

J. Jones
General Manager
Industrial Testing Services
122 Main Street
Indianapolis, Indiana 12345

Dear J. Jones:

In response to your need for a Nondestructive Tester, as listed in the *Indianapolis Star*, I would appreciate the opportunity to evaluate my background and qualifications with you. There is a match between the listed requirements of the position and my experiences, skills and education.

As a Nondestructive Tester, I have the experience and knowledge to use liquid penetrates, magnetic particles, x-ray, ultrasonic and eddy current. I am proficient in the use of lab equipment. I can produce quality inspections and documentations and contribute to the safety, profitability and success of your organization.

I welcome the opportunity to discuss any possibilities with you.

Sincerely,

Jane or John Doe

Enclosed: Resume

Answering an Advertisement *without* a Person or Company Name.

JANE or JOHN DOE
123 Main Street
AnyTown, AnyState AnyZip
000-000-0000
email@abc.com

Current Date

P. O. Box 123
Indianapolis, Indiana 12345

Nondestructive Tester:

In response to your need for a Nondestructive Tester, as listed in the *Indianapolis Star*, I would appreciate the opportunity to evaluate my background and qualifications with you. There is a match between the listed requirements of the position and my experiences, skills and education.

As a Nondestructive Tester, I have the experience and knowledge to use liquid penetrates, magnetic particles, x-ray, ultrasonic and eddy current. I am proficient in the use of lab equipment. I can produce quality inspections and documentations and contribute to the safety, profitability and success of your organization.

I welcome the opportunity to discuss any possibilities with you.

Sincerely,

Jane or John Doe

Enclosed: Resume

THE COVER LETTER

(Companies who are not advertising)

When sending these cold call resumes, obtain the company names, human resources or department heads names, addresses and telephone numbers from the library. Publications, such as: *Standard & Poors*, *Harris Industrial Directory*, *Thomas Register* or the *Chamber of Commerce* will have the information necessary to mail your resume. Typically, these publications will profile the company, informing you who they are, what they produce, how they distribute, the key people, and the company's gross income. Your state employment office will also assist you with this information. If the company does not list a human resource person, send it to the president or department head to whom you are applying.

In addition to the above information, you should maintain a list of the companies and the person to whom you are mailing your resumes – don't forget the telephone number for follow-up.

Mail only five resumes at a time. Follow-up by phone to the person to whom you mailed your resume. If you obtain a negative response, ask if they know of any company who is hiring in their

area. Be sure to get a person's name, phone number, company name and address. Ask if you may use their name as a referral when contacting the new company. Add them to your next mailing.

THE COVER LETTER (SAMPLE)

(Sending resumes to companies
who are not advertising)

JANE or JOHN DOE
123 Main Street
AnyTown, AnyState AnyZip
000-000-0000
email@abc.com

Current Date

J. Jones
Personnel Director
XYZ Corporation
123 Main Street
Anytown, Anystate 12345

Dear Mr. or Ms. Jones:

If your company has a current need for a Machine Set-up Operator, I would like the opportunity to evaluate my background and qualifications with you.

As a Machinist, I have the experience to set-up and operate machine tools, such as lathes, milling machines, boring machines, and grinders to machine metallic and nonmetallic work pieces according to specifications, tooling instructions, and standard charts, applying knowledge of machine methods. I am proficient in the use of CNC equipment and precision measuring instruments. I can read blueprints, working drawings and specifications.

I can produce quality parts or products and contribute to the production, profitability, safety and success of your organization. I welcome the opportunity to discuss any possibilities with you.

Sincerely,

Jane or John Doe

Enclosure: Resume

You have been invited to an interview. You are now going to receive...

...THE APPLICATION

There are thousands of application forms. The thing to remember – print neatly, answer all questions truthfully, if a question does not pertain, simply write N/A.

Have a list of (3) character references with their names, title, address and phone numbers. Also, have a list of business references with the same information as above. Be sure to ask for their permission before using their names. It is also wise to provide the references with your resume.

Be sure you are correct with your education information. It is noted that a high percentage of applicants are not correct with their education listings. Also, if you have a GED, do not be discouraged – most companies look at a person who obtains a GED as a good prospective employee.

Don't fudge on your income. Again, a large majority of people inflates their income on the application. Be truthful.

A lot of companies are also checking credit before hiring. They look at your credit history as a gauge to your character.

The information you provide on the application should coincide with your resume.

Print neatly!

THE INTERVIEW

You have emailed your resume and cover letter to the prospective employer. In addition, you mailed a follow-up original. You provided a salary history, if requested.

Practice with your friends, family members or business associates in answering their hardball interviewing questions. The more you practice, the more you will be spontaneous in answering. Practice answering in a positive and truthful manner. Remember, you have only one chance with the employer. He will want to know if you have done your homework in knowing about his company and the job for which you are applying.

The employer has phoned (or emailed) you and invited you for an interview. He will suggest a date and time. If that is not possible for you, due to other commitments, ask if it can be changed to another time. Always, give two times, if possible: Would 9am on Tuesday or 2pm on Thursday be a good time for you? Interviews may take place before or after their work hour. Be flexible!

If the employer has not contacted you within a week, follow-up with a phone call. Ask if they had received your resume. In some cases, emails are not received. You would like to know the status.

Typically, there are three types of interviews:

<u>Telephone</u>: The telephone is a screening call to determine if you are qualified for the position. You should provide the interviewer with your skills and knowledge as it relates to the job you are seeking. Be positive and provide the answers to the questions. At the end of the interview, ask when you can meet with the interviewer. Get the interviewer's name, telephone number and address where the meeting will take place.

Remember – first impressions are lasting. Don't overdo the cologne, as some people are allergic to strong odors. Leave the body piercing at home.

When going to the interview, dress for the part for which you are applying. It is impressive to see a candidate in freshly ironed / pressed clothing and shined shoes. Hire a baby sitter. You should have your resume and the other pertinent information you brought for filling in the application. Be calm. Visualize you are talking to your best friend.

Do not discuss salary until the interviewer brings it up. Answer the salary question with a question: Typically, what do you start a new employee who has my skills and experiences? He may want to start you at more than you had expected.

***Personal Interview*: This is a one-on-one interview. It may take place in an office, a conference room, cafeteria, or any place where you and the interviewer will be comfortable. The interviewer will ask general questions in order to relax you. Interviewers also become nervous. Maybe, they do not have the knowledge you have regarding the position and the skills involved. Communicate that you are flexible (work whenever needed), productive, and believe in quality output. You are a team player.**

Body language is important. Look the interviewer in the eye. When answering questions, don't look around, twiddle your thumbs, pinch your lips, swing your legs, etc. Sit erect and keep eye contact.

At the conclusion of the interview, ask when you can start! When you ask that question, _do not speak_ until the interviewer has answered your question.

<u>*Group Interview*</u>: The group interview may have 2 to 5 people. It is important not to get nervous. Look at this group as your family. Be relaxed (but do not slouch), be confident and positive. Look into the questioner's eye and answer the questions. They may ask questions requiring some thought or how you solve problems. Take your time and answer. The group interview is the same as a one-to-one interview – only multiple people with different skills will be asking the questions. Answer each one directly.

It is important to get the name of the group leader. Obtain his/her business card so you may write a thank you letter.

When the interview is over. Ask: <u>*When may I start my new job?*</u>

Don't forget to send the 'Thank You' Letter! The thank you letter should be sent the same day, next day or hand delivered.

ADDRESSING THE INCARCERATION ISSUE

I have interviewed many people who were incarcerated due to a mistake they made in the past. They made restitution for their poor judgment and its time to face the interviewer.

It is best that the resume does not show the time of incarceration (see the Apprentice Plumber resume, and Chef pages 10 and 13). Rather, if you are called for the interview, tell the truth. Many interviewers will want to know the circumstance of the judgment. They may not want to hire you if the offense was really bad. Regardless, you must look the interviewer in the eye and tell him that you are remorseful of this event in your life and that you made a mistake in judgment – if offered this opportunity, you will be an excellent long-term employee for his company.

Have references or letters that will verify and support your integrity.

Unfortunately, you may have to accept a job of lesser value, but if you can take a position and continue to look for something better, you will have a chance of succeeding. Don't give up!

Sixty-six percent (66%) of new jobs are with small companies. These are excellent employers.

The 'Thank You' Letter

JANE or JOHN DOE
123 Main Street
AnyTown, AnyState AnyZip
000-000-0000
email@abc.com

Current Date

J. Jones
Personnel Director
XYZ Corporation
123 Main Street
Anytown, Anystate 12345

Dear Mr. or Ms. Jones:

Thank you for giving me the opportunity to interview with you (and your staff – if it was a group interview) for the position of Machine Operator.

I look forward to being a long-term employee with your organization. I am reliable, productive, flexible and believe in quality output.

You will be pleased with my performance.

Sincerely,

Jane or John Doe

Note: *Employers state that twenty percent (20%) of people who sent a 'thank you' note or letter were hired.*

Maximize you efforts! It works.

56

…IN CONCLUSION,

it is important to obtain that job you want for the rest of your working career. A job that you can be proud of, and one that you look forward to each working day. In order to find that career position, and if not known, you should be tested to determine your career path - based on your interests, aptitude, skills and values. These tests are typically given by your state employment office and are at no cost to you.

If you are computer literate, this is good. If not, I would suggest your attending a night course and learn the basis. It's not that difficult and it will prepare you for that career position.

When you know what career position you want, prepare the resume and cover letter as outlined in this book – don't leave out a step. The objective is to obtain an interview and get the job.

Use those publications at the library to determine to whom you want to send your resume and cover letter. Make notes about the company so you may communicate your knowledge about the company to the interviewer. Don't forget the small businesses, as they have competitive pay structures and benefits.

K. B. McIntosh

Finding a job or career position is a full time chore. Success is obtained by persevering. Good Luck!